EXPLORING NATURE

BIG CATS

Examine the fearsome feline world of lions, tigers, cheetahs
and leopards, in more than 190 pictures

Rhonda Klevansky • Consultant: Dr Nigel Dunstone

ARMADILLO

C O N

This edition is published by Armadillo, an imprint of Anness Publishing Ltd, 108 Great Russell Street, London WC1B 3NA; info@anness.com

www.annesspublishing.com

Anness Publishing has a picture agency outlet for images for publishing, promotions or advertising. Please visit www.practicalpictures.com for more information.

© Anness Publishing Ltd 2014

Publisher: Joanna Lorenz
Project Editors: Charlotte Hurdman, Richard McGinlay
Designers: Traffika Publishing Ltd, Mirjana Nociar
Picture Researchers: Elizabeth Walsh, Kay Rowley
Illustrators: David Webb, Vanessa Card, Peter Bull
Production Controller: Rosie Anness
With thanks to Nicole Pearson for her work on this title

Manufacturer: Anness Publishing Ltd, 108 Great Russell Street, London WC1B 3NA, England
For Product Tracking go to: www.annesspublishing.com/tracking
Batch: 6779-23071-1127

T E N T S

What is a Cat?

Cats are native to every continent except Australia and Antarctica. All cats are mammals with fine fur that is often beautifully marked. They are skilled hunters and killers with strong agile bodies, acute senses and sharp teeth and claws. Cats are stealthy and intelligent animals and many are solitary and very secretive. Although cats vary in size from the domestic (house) cat to the huge Siberian tiger, they all belong to the same family, the Felidae. This means that both wild and domestic cats look alike and behave in very similar ways. In all, there are 38 different species of cat.

▲ **LONG TAIL**
A cat's long tail helps it to balance as it runs. Cats also use their tails to signal their feelings to other cats.

All cats have short, rounded heads.

Whiskers help a cat feel its surroundings.

The body of a cat is muscular and supple, with a broad, powerful chest.

▲ **BIG BITE**
As this tiger yawns it reveals its sharp teeth and strong jaws that can give a lethal bite. Cats use their long, curved canine teeth for killing prey.

▲ **BIG CATS**
Cats are very specialized meat-eaters. They are the perfect carnivore, with excellent hearing and eyesight. Their curved, razor-sharp claws, used for catching and holding prey, are retractable. This means they can be pulled into the paws to protect them when running. The hair covering a cat's paws and surrounding the pads helps it move silently.

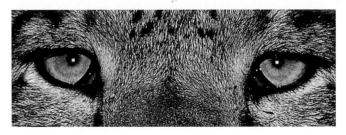

▲ **NIGHT SIGHT**

The pupils (dark middles) of cats' eyes close to a slit or small circle during the day to keep out the glare. At night they open up to let in as much light as possible. This enables a cat to see at night as well as during the day.

The Lion and the Saint
St Jerome was a Christian scholar who lived from about AD 331 to 420. According to legend, he found an injured lion in the desert with a thorn in its paw. Instead of attacking him, the lion befriended the saint when he removed the thorn. St Jerome is often shown with a lion sitting at his feet.

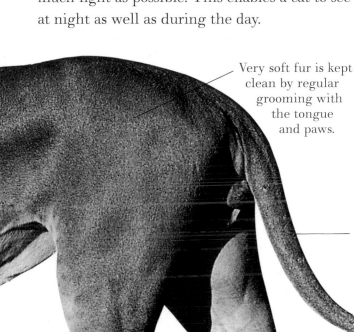

Very soft fur is kept clean by regular grooming with the tongue and paws.

A long tail helps the cat to balance when it runs and leaps on prey.

Did you know? Some Arctic cultures believe that cats represent the spirits of the dead.

Cats walk on their toes, not on the whole foot.

Large ears draw in sounds.

CATS' EARS ▶

A cat's ears are set high on its head. This gives a keen hunter the best possible chance of picking up sounds. The ears have a rounded shape, which enables sounds to be picked up from many directions. Cats can also rotate their ears to face towards the source of a sound.

The Big Cats

Scientists classify (arrange) the members of the cat family into related groups. The two main groups are small cats (the domestic cat and many wild cats) and the big cats (the tiger, lion, leopard, snow leopard and jaguar). The clouded leopard and the cheetah are each grouped separately, but many people regard them as big cats. Big cats differ from small cats not only because of their size. Big cats can roar, but small cats cannot. Small cats purr. They have a special bone, the hyoid, at the base of their tongues that enables them to breathe and purr at the same time. Big cats have elastic cartilage instead and can only purr when they breathe out. The puma is in fact a very large small cat. It is discussed here because of its size.

▲ LION
The lion is the only social cat and lives in a family group called a pride. Adult male lions, unlike other big cats, have a long, thick mane of hair. Female lions do not have manes.

▲ PUMA
The puma is also called the cougar or mountain lion. Although it is about the same size as a leopard, a puma is considered a small cat because it can purr. Pumas live in North and South America.

◄ CHEETAH
The tall cheetah is built like a slim athlete and is able to chase prey at great speed. Cheetahs are different from other cats in that they have retractable claws, but no sheaths to cover them. It was once thought that cheetahs were related to dogs, but scientists now think that their closest cousins are pumas.

▲ LEOPARD

The leopard is built for bursts of speed and for climbing trees. Heavier than a cheetah, this cat is not so large and bulky as a tiger or a lion. Its spotted coat helps to hide the cat as it hunts in wooded grassland. Black leopards are called panthers. They are the same species, but their spots are hidden.

▲ SNOW LEOPARD

Snow leopards are a different species from true leopards. These rare cats have very thick coats to keep them warm in the high mountains of central Asia. They have very long tails, which help them to balance as they leap from rock to rock in their mountainous surroundings.

▼ JAGUAR

The jaguar is sometimes confused with a leopard, but it is stockier and not so agile. It lives throughout South America in forested habitats where it needs strength to climb rather than speed to run.

▲ TIGER

The most powerful and largest of all the big cats is the tiger. A tiger reaches on average a length of over 2m/6½ft and weighs about 230kg/500lb. The biggest tigers live in the snowy forests of Siberia in Russia. A few tigers also live in tropical forest reserves and swamps in Asia.

Did you know? Although lions are called the king of the jungle, they do not live there.

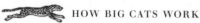

Bones and Teeth

The skeleton of a cat gives it its shape and has 230 bones (a human has about 206). Its short and round skull is joined to the spine (backbone), which supports the body. Vertebrae (bones of the spine) protect the spinal cord, which is the main nerve cable in the body. The ribs are joined to the spine, forming a cage that protects a cat's heart and lungs. Cats' teeth are designed for killing and chewing. Wild cats have to be very careful not to damage their teeth, because with broken teeth they would quickly die from starvation.

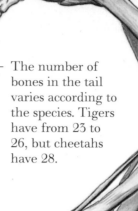

Spine

A big, flexible rib cage has 13 ribs.

The number of bones in the tail varies according to the species. Tigers have from 23 to 26, but cheetahs have 28.

The bones of a cat's powerful hind legs are longer than the front leg bones.

▲ THE FRAME

The powerfully built skeleton of a tiger is similar to all cats' skeletons. Cats have short necks with seven compressed vertebrae. These help to streamline and balance the cat so that it can achieve greater speeds. All cats have slightly different shoulder bones. A cheetah has long shoulder bones to which sprinting muscles are attached. A leopard, however, has short shoulder bones and thicker, tree-climbing muscles.

◄ CANINES AND CARNASSIALS

A tiger reveals its fearsome teeth. Its long, curved canines are adapted to fit between the neck bones of its prey to break the spinal cord. Like all carnivores, cats have strong back teeth, called carnassials. These do most of the cutting by tearing off pieces of meat.

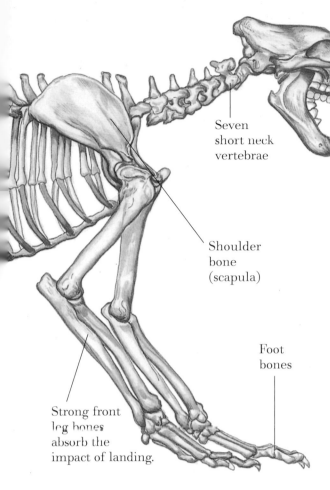

Seven
short neck
vertebrae

Shoulder
bone
(scapula)

Foot
bones

Strong front
leg bones
absorb the
impact of landing.

LANDING FEET ▶
As it falls, this cat
twists its supple,
flexible spine to make
sure its feet will be
in the right place for
landing. Cats almost
always land on their
feet when they fall.
This helps them to
avoid injury as they
leap on prey or jump
from a tree.

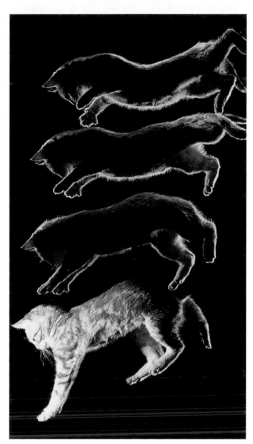

▼ CHEWING ON A BONE
Ravenous lions feast on the carcass of their latest
kill. Cats' jaws are hinged so that their jaw bones
can move only from side to side, not up and down.
Because of this, cats eat on one side of their mouths
at a time and often tilt their heads when they eat.

▼ CAT SKULL
Like all cats' skulls, this tiger's skull has a
high crown at the back giving lots of space
for its strong neck muscles. Big eye sockets
allow it to see well to the sides as well as to
the front. Its short jaws can open wide
to deliver a powerful bite.

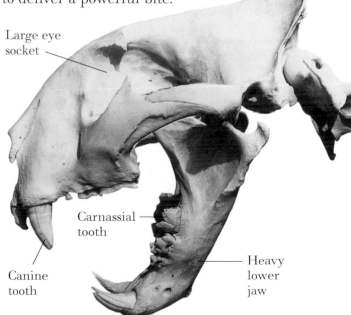

Large eye
socket

Carnassial
tooth

Canine
tooth

Heavy
lower
jaw

Muscles and Claws

Both inside and out, cats are designed to be skilled hunters and killers. Thick back and shoulder muscles help them to be excellent jumpers and climbers. Sharp, curved claws that grow from all of their digits (toes) are their weapons. One of the digits on a cat's front foot is called the dew claw. This is held off the ground to keep it sharp and ready to hold prey. Cats are warm-blooded, which means that their bodies stay at the same temperature no matter how hot or cold the weather is. The fur on their skin keeps them warm when conditions are cold. When it is hot, cats cool down by sweating through their noses and paw pads.

Heracles and the Nemean Lion
The mythical Greek hero Heracles was the son of the god Zeus and tremendously strong. As a young man he committed a terrible crime. Part of his punishment was to kill the Nemean lion. The lion had impenetrable skin and could not be killed with arrows or spears. Heracles chased the lion into a cave and strangled it with his hands. He wore its skin as a shield and its head as a helmet.

▼ **KNOCKOUT CLAWS**

Cheetahs have well-developed dew claws that stick out from their front legs. They use these claws to knock down prey before grabbing its throat or muzzle to strangle it. Other cats use their dew claws to grip while climbing or to hold on to prey. Cats have five claws, including the dew claw, on their front paws. On their back paws, they have only four claws.

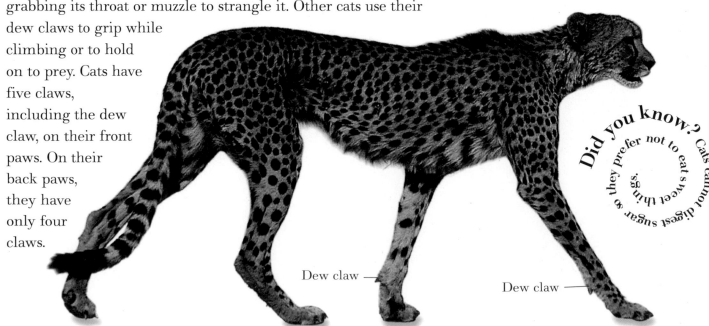

Dew claw →

Dew claw →

Did you know? Cats cannot digest sugar, so they prefer not to eat sweet things.

▲ TIGER CLAW

This is the extended claw of a tiger. Cats' claws are made of keratin, just like human fingernails. They need to be kept sharp all the time.

Underneath the skin, a lion's muscular body follows the lines of its skeleton.

▲ MUSCLES FOR KILLING

Cats have very strong shoulder and neck muscles for attacking prey. The muscles also absorb some of the impact when the cat pounces.

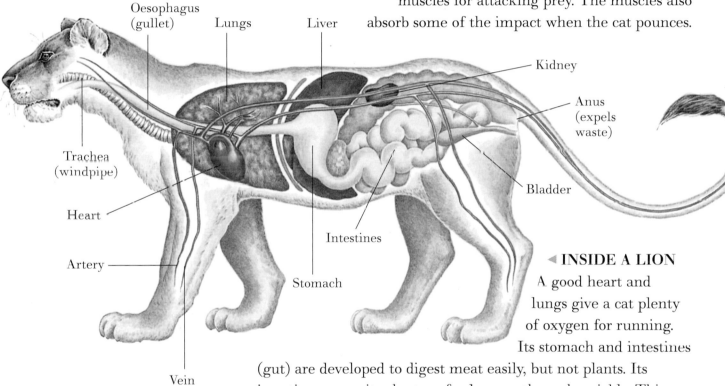

Oesophagus (gullet)

Lungs

Liver

Kidney

Anus (expels waste)

Trachea (windpipe)

Bladder

Heart

Intestines

Artery

Stomach

Vein

◄ INSIDE A LION

A good heart and lungs give a cat plenty of oxygen for running. Its stomach and intestines (gut) are developed to digest meat easily, but not plants. Its intestines are quite short, so food passes through quickly. This means as soon as it needs more food, a cat is light enough to run and pounce. However, once a lion has had a big meal, it does not need to eat again for several days.

CLAW PROTECTION ▶

Cats retract (pull back) their claws into fleshy sheaths to protect them. This prevents them from getting blunt or damaged. Only cheetahs lack sheaths.

Flexed muscle

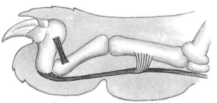

Sheathed claw is protected by a fleshy covering.

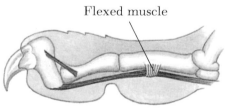

The claw is unsheathed when a muscle tightens.

Sight and Sound

To hunt well and not be seen or heard by prey or enemies, cats use their senses of sight, sound and touch. Cats' eyesight is excellent. Their eyes are adapted for night vision, but they can also see well in the day. Cats' eyes are big compared to the size of their heads. They have good binocular vision, which allows them accurately to judge how far away objects are. At night, cats see in black and white. They can see colours in the day, but not so well as humans can. Cats have very good hearing, much better than a human's. They can hear small animals rustling through the grass or even moving around in their burrows underground.

Did you know? A cat's pupils open wide when it is frightened and close up when it is angry.

▲ **CAUGHT IN BRIGHT LIGHT**
Cats' eyes are very sensitive to light. During the day in bright light, the pupils of the eyes close right down, letting in only as much light as is needed to see well. A domestic cat's pupils close down to slits, while most big cats' pupils close to tiny circles.

◄ **GLOWING EYES**
Behind the retinas (light sensitive areas) in this leopard's eyes is a reflecting layer called the tapetum lucidum. This helps to absorb extra light in the dark. When light shines into the eyes at night, the reflectors glow.

PREY IN SIGHT ▶

As it stalks through the long grass, a lion must pounce at just the right moment if it is to catch its prey. Binocular vision helps the cat to judge when to strike. Because its eyes are set slightly apart at the front of the head, their field of view overlaps. This enables a cat to judge the position of its prey exactly.

▲ **ROUND-EYED**

This puma's rounded pupils have closed down in daylight. In dim light, the pupils will expand wide to let in as much light as possible.

SHARP EARS ▶

Cats' ears are designed for them to hear very well. This Siberian lynx lives in snowy forests where the sound is often muffled. It has specially-shaped, big ears to catch as much sound as possible.

Large earflaps concentrate sound waves deep into each ear.

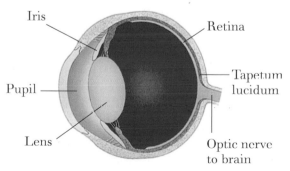

Iris

Retina

Pupil

Tapetum lucidum

Lens

Optic nerve to brain

▲ **INSIDE THE EYE**

The lens focuses light rays to produce a sharp image on the retina. Impulses from the retina are carried to the brain by the optic nerve. Cats have a membrane that can be pulled over the surface of the eye to keep out dirt and dust.

Touching, Tasting and Smelling

Like all animals, cats feel things with nerves in their skin, but they have another important touching tool – whiskers. These long, stiff hairs on the face have very sensitive nerve endings at their roots. Some whiskers are for protection. Anything brushing against the whiskers above a cat's eyes will make it blink. Cats use smell and taste to communicate with each other. A cat's tongue is a useful tool and its nose is very sensitive. Thin, curled bones in the nose carry scents inwards to smell receptors. Unlike most animals, cats have special places on the roofs of their mouths to distinguish scents, especially of other cats.

▲ **TONGUE TOOL**
A leopard curls the tip of its tongue like a spoon to lap up water. After several laps it will drink the water in one gulp. As well as drinking, the tongue is used for tasting, scraping meat off a carcass and grooming.

◄ **ROUGH TONGUE**
A tiger's bright pink tongue has a very rough surface. Cats' tongues are covered with small spikes called papillae. The papillae point backwards and are used by the cat, together with its teeth, to strip meat off bones. Around the edge and at the back of the tongue are taste buds. Cats cannot taste sweet things, but can actively recognize pure water.

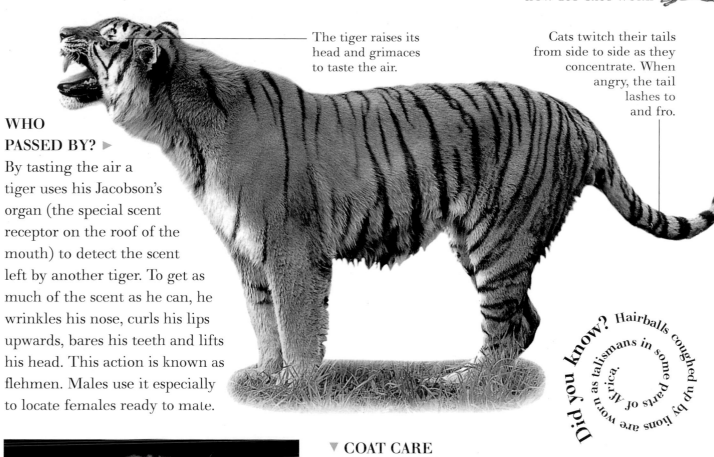

The tiger raises its head and grimaces to taste the air.

Cats twitch their tails from side to side as they concentrate. When angry, the tail lashes to and fro.

WHO PASSED BY? ▶

By tasting the air a tiger uses his Jacobson's organ (the special scent receptor on the roof of the mouth) to detect the scent left by another tiger. To get as much of the scent as he can, he wrinkles his nose, curls his lips upwards, bares his teeth and lifts his head. This action is known as flehmen. Males use it especially to locate females ready to mate.

Did you know? Hairballs coughed up by lions are worn as talismans in some parts of Africa.

▲ THE CATS' WHISKERS

This snow leopard's face is surrounded by sensitive whiskers. Cats use their whiskers to judge how far away objects are. The most important whiskers are on the sides of the face. These help a cat to feel its way in the dark, or when it is walking through tall grass.

▼ COAT CARE

The long, rough tongue of a lion makes a very good comb. It removes loose hairs and combs the fur flat and straight. Cats wipe their faces, coats and paws clean. They need to keep well groomed and spend a lot of time looking after their fur. Hair swallowed by grooming is spat out as hairballs.

15

Spots and Stripes

A cat's fur coat protects its skin and keeps it warm. The coat's coloration and patterns help to camouflage (hide) the cat as it hunts prey. Wild cats' coats have two layers — an undercoat of short soft fur and an outercoat of tougher, longer hairs, called guard hairs. Together these two layers insulate the cat from extreme cold or extren heat. Some guard hairs are sensitive and help a cat to feel its way. Cats have loose skin, making it difficult for an attacker to get a good grip and helping to prevent injury. The appearance of a wild cat's coat depends on where it lives.

▲ **TIGER IN THE GRASS**
The stripes of a tiger's coat are the perfect camouflage for an animal that needs to prowl around in long grass. The shades and patterns help to make the cat almost invisible as it stalks its prey. These markings are also very effective in a leafy jungle where the dappled light makes stripes of light and shade.

Did you know? Domestic cats have a wider range of coloration and markings than wild cats.

◄ **KING OF THE HILL**
King cheetahs were once thought to be different from other cheetahs. They have longer fur, are darker and have spots on their backs that join up to form stripes. Even so, they are the same species. All cheetahs have distinctive tear stripes running from the corners of their eyes down beside their muzzles.

▲ NON-IDENTICAL TWINS

Many big cats of the same species vary in appearance, depending on where they live. These two leopard cubs are twins, but one has a much darker, blackish coat. Black leopards are called panthers. (Black jaguars and even pumas are also sometimes called panthers.) Some leopards live deep in the shadows of the forest, where darker fur allows them to hide more easily. Panthers are most common in Asia.

▼ SPOT THE DIFFERENCE

Spots, stripes or blotches break up the outline of a cat's body. This helps it to blend in with the shadows made by the leaves of bushes and trees or the lines of tall grass. In the dappled light of a forest or in the long grass of the savanna, cats are very well hidden indeed.

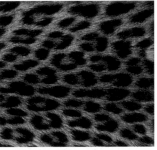
A leopard's spots are in fact small rosettes.

The tiger has distinctive black stripes.

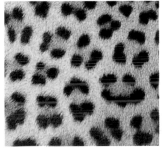
A jaguar has rosettes with a central spot of yellow.

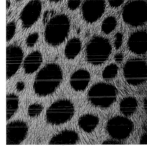
The cheetah has lots of spots and no rosettes.

◄ WHITE FOR SNOW

A snow leopard has a shaggy, off-white coat with darker spots. This coloration helps the snow leopard to stay well hidden in the rocky, mountainous terrain where it lives. It moves around early in the morning or late afternoon, blending with its habitat as it looks for prey.

A snow leopard's pale, thick coat has dark irregular spots and streaks. This helps it to hide between the rocks and snow.

On the Move

Cats run and jump easily and gracefully. They have flexible spines and long, strong hind legs. With long, bouncy strides, they can cover a lot of ground very quickly. Big cats are not good long-distance runners, they are sprinters and pouncers. They use their long tails for balance when climbing trees and running fast. All cats can swim very well, but some do not like the water and will only swim to escape danger. Others, such as tigers and jaguars, live near water and often swim to hunt their prey.

▲ **THRILL OF THE CHASE**
A lion chases its prey through the scrub. When lions stalk, run and pounce, they make use of their flexible backs, strong back legs, powerful chests and cushioning pads under their paws. Cats' back legs are especially powerful. They provide the major thrust for running. Cats can outpace their prey over short distances before launching into a final jump.

◄ **TREE-CLIMBING CAT**
Leopards spend a lot of time in trees and are designed for climbing. They have very powerful chests and front legs. Their shoulder blades are positioned to the side to make them better climbers.
A leopard can leap 3m/10ft without difficulty and, in exceptional circumstances, can leap over 6m/20ft.

18

◄ **SOFT PADDING**

The thick pads under a lion's paw are like cushions. They allow the lion to move very quietly and also act as shock absorbers for running and jumping. Hidden between the pads and fur are the lion's claws, tucked away safely until they are needed.

GRACE AND AGILITY ►

A bobcat leaps with great agility off a rock. All cats have flexible backs and short collarbones to help make their bodies stronger for jumping off things. Bobcats are similar to lynxes. Both cats have an extensive coating of fur on their feet to give them extra warmth. The fur also prevents them from slipping on icy rocks.

Did you know? In the 16th century, rich people kept cheetahs as hunting animals like dogs.

As it leaps, a bobcat pinpoints its landing position. The front feet land separately in quick succession.

◄ **KEEPING COOL CAT**

A Bengal tiger swims gracefully across a river. Many tigers live in warm climates, such as India and South-east Asia. As well as swimming to get from one place to another, they often look for pools of water to bathe in during the heat of the day. They are one of the few cats that actively enjoy being in or near water. Tigers are superb swimmers and can easily cross a lake 5km/3 miles wide.

19

Focus on the

A cheetah can run at 115kph/70mph over short distances – a speed equivalent to a fast car. This makes it the world's fastest land animal. The cheetah's body is fine-tuned for speed. It has wide nostrils to breathe in as much oxygen as possible and specially adapted paws for running fast. Most cheetahs today live in east and southern Africa, with a small number living in Asia – in Iran and Pakistan. They live in many different kinds of habitats, from open grassland to thick bush and even in desert-like environments.

1 A pair of cheetahs creep up stealthily on a herd of antelope. Cheetahs hunt their prey by slinking towards the herd, holding their heads low. Cheetahs are not pouncing killers, like other cats. Instead, they pull down their prey after a very fast chase. In order to waste as little energy as possible, cheetahs plan their attack first. They pick out their target before starting the chase.

2 The cheetah begins its chase as the herd of antelope starts to move. It can accelerate from walking pace to around 70kph/40mph in two seconds. Cheetahs have retractable claws, but unlike other cats they have no protective sheaths. The uncovered claws act like the spikes on the bottom of track shoes, helping the cheetah to grip as it runs. Ridges on their paw pads also help to improve grip.

3 At top speed a cheetah makes full use of its flexible spine and lean, supple body. A cheetah's legs are very long and slender compared to its body. It can cover several metres in a single bound.

Hunting Cheetah

4 As the cheetah closes in on the herd, the antelope spring in all directions. The cheetah changes direction without slowing down. If a cheetah does not catch its prey within about 400m/1,300 ft, it has to give up the chase. Cheetahs usually hunt in the morning or late in the afternoon, when it is not too hot. They have short lifespans in the wild, because their speed declines with age, making it difficult to catch prey.

5 As the cheetah closes in on its prey it may have to make several sharp turns to keep up. The cheetah's long tail gives it excellent balance as it turns. The cheetah knocks its victim off balance with a swipe of its front paw. It uses its big dew claw to pull the victim to the ground.

6 Once the prey animal is down, the cheetah grabs the victim's throat. A sharp bite suffocates the antelope. Cheetahs are not strong enough to kill by biting through the spinal cord in the prey's neck like other cats. The cheetah will hang on to the victim's throat until the antelope is dead.

Communication

All big cats communicate with one another. They tell each other how old they are, whether they are male or female, what mood they are in and where they live. Cats communicate by signals such as smells, scratches and sounds. The smells come from urine and from scent glands. Cats have scent glands on their heads and chins, between their toes and at the base of their tails. Every time they rub against something, they transfer their special smell. Cats make many different sounds. Scientists know that cats speak to each other, but still do not understand much about their language. Cats also communicate using body language. They use their ears to signal their mood and twitch their tails to show if they are excited or agitated.

▲ A MIGHTY ROAR

The lion's roar is the loudest sound cats make. It is loud enough for all the nearby lions to hear. Lions roar after sunset, following a kill and when they have finished eating. Lions make at least nine different sounds. They also grunt to each other as they move around.

HISSING LEOPARD ▶

An angry leopard hisses at an enemy. Cats hiss and spit when they feel threatened or when they are fighting an enemy. The position of a cat's ears also signals its intentions. When a cat is about to attack, it flattens its ears back against its neck.

▲ EAR SIGNALS

Many wild cats, such as this tiger, have white markings on the back of their ears. They turn their ears to show the markings to an enemy when they are angry.

▲ MARKS FOR SHOW

Cats like to scratch things to clean their claws and stretch their limbs. At the same time they leave a scented mark for others to both see and smell. When this lioness scratches, she leaves her own personal scent from the glands between her toes on the scratch marks.

▲ CAT SPRAY

A king cheetah marks its territory by spraying urine at points along its trails. Scent marks left by a male tell other males to stay away. The scent left by a female will tell a male passing through her range if she is ready to mate.

BABY TALK ▶

Mothers talk to their cubs a lot. The sounds are quiet so that enemies do not hear. The softest and safest sound of all is purring.

Did you know? When they are close together, lions chirrup, meow and yowl to each other.

Hunting Prey

All cats, big and small, are carnivores – they eat meat. Their bodies are not designed to digest plants. Big cats must hunt down and kill their own food. Most big cats, however, are only too happy to eat someone else's meal and steal kills from other animals whenever they can. Cheetahs are an exception and eat only animals they have killed themselves. To catch and kill their food, big cats must hunt. Some, like cheetahs, patrol their territory, looking for prey. Others, such as jaguars, hide in wait and then ambush their victims. Many cats, such as leopards, do both.

King Solomon
Solomon ruled Israel in the 900s BC *and was reputed to be a very wise ruler. His throne was carved with lions because of his admiration for these big cats who killed only out of necessity. In law, if a man was said to have fallen into a lion's den, it was not proof of his death.*

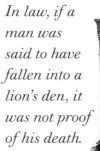

◀ **THE MAIN COURSE**
A big lion can kill large, powerful animals such as this buffalo. A big cat usually attacks from behind or from the side. If the prey is too big to grab right away, the cat will knock it off balance, hold on to it and bite into its neck.

CHOOSING A MEAL ▶
A herd of antelope and zebra grazes while keeping watch on a lioness crouched in the grass. She lies as close to the ground as possible, waiting to pounce. Finally, when focused on a victim, she will bring her hind legs back into position and dart forwards.

▲ WARTHOG SPECIAL

Four cheetahs surround an injured warthog. The mother cheetah is teaching her three cubs hunting techniques. The cheetah on the right is trying a left paw side swipe, while another tries using its dew claw. Cheetahs love to eat warthogs, but also catch antelope and smaller animals.

▲ CAT AND MOUSE

A recently killed capybara (a large rodent) makes a tasty meal for a jaguar. Jaguars often catch their food in water, such as fish and turtles. On land they hunt armadillos, deer, opossums, skunks, snakes, squirrels, tortoises and monkeys.

Did you know? Cheetahs will only chase prey if it runs. If it stops, so does the cheetah.

SLOW FOOD ▶

If a lion has not been able to hunt successfully for a while, it will eat small creatures such as this tortoise. Lions usually hunt big animals, such as antelope, wildebeest, warthogs, giraffe, buffalo, bush pigs and baboons. They work together in a group to hunt large prey.

Killing Prey

The way a big cat kills its prey depends on the size of the cat and the size of its meal. If the prey is small with a bite-sized neck, it will be killed with a bite through the spinal cord. If the prey has a bite-sized head, the cat will use its powerful jaws to crush the back of its skull. Large prey is killed by biting its throat and suffocating it. Lions often hunt together and use a combined effort to kill large prey. One lion may grab the prey's throat to suffocate it, while other lions attack from behind.

Did you know? Lions try to flip porcupines on to their backs to avoid the sharp spines.

▼ OLD AGE
When big cats get old or injured it is very difficult for them to hunt. They will eventually die from starvation. This lion from the Kalahari Desert in South Africa is old and thin. It has been weakened by hunger.

◀ FAIR GAME
A warthog is a small, delicious meal for a cheetah. The bigger the cat, the bigger its prey. A cheetah is quite a light cat, so to kill an animal the cheetah first knocks it over, then bites the prey's neck to suffocate it.

▲ A DEADLY EMBRACE
A lioness immobilizes a struggling wildebeest by biting its windpipe and suffocating it to death. Lions are very strong animals. A lion weighing 150–250kg/330–550lb can kill a buffalo more than twice its weight. Female lions do most of the hunting for their pride.

◀ SECRET STASH

A cheetah carrying off its prey, a young gazelle, to a safe place. Once it has killed, a cheetah will check the area to make sure it is secure before feeding. It drags the carcass to a covered place in the bushes. Here it can eat its meal hidden from enemies. Cheetahs are often driven off and robbed of their kills by hyenas and jackals or even other big cats.

A SOLID MEAL ▶

These cheetahs will devour as much of this antelope as they can. Big cats lie on the ground and hold their food with their forepaws when they eat. When they have satisfied their hunger, cheetahs cover up or hide the carcass with grass, leaves or whatever is available in order to save it for later.

LIONS' FEAST ▶

A pride of lions gather around their kill, a zebra. They eat quickly before any scavenging hyenas and vultures can steal the meat. Each lion has its place in the pride. Even if they are very hungry, they must wait until it is their turn to eat. Usually the dominant male lion eats first.

27

Focus on the Lone

Leopards are one of the most widespread of all the big cats, but are also the most secretive. They live in many different habitats throughout Africa and southern Asia, in open, rocky country as well as in forests. Not much is known about them because they are nocturnal animals, coming out to hunt at night. They sometimes creep up on prey on the ground, then pounce. At other times they ambush their prey from a tree.

CAT NAP
Leopards usually sleep all day in a tree, especially when it is very hot. Their spotted coats are excellent camouflage in the patchwork of light and shade in the forest. They are so good that, when they are resting, they are especially hard to see.

LONE LEOPARD
Leopards are loners. They come together only when a female signals to a male that she is ready to mate. After mating they separate again. The mother brings up the cubs until they are able to fend for themselves.

Leopard

BRUTE STRENGTH
A leopard drags its dead victim across the ground. Leopards have strong jaws, chests and front legs so that they can move an animal as big as themselves.

AMBUSH
Leopards like to ambush prey. They climb on to a low branch and wait for an animal to walk underneath. Then they jump down and grab it. The leopard uses its great strength to drag its victim high up into the tree. Prey includes pigs, antelope, monkeys, dogs and many other animals.

TOP MEAL
A leopard has dragged its kill up into a tree. This is to prevent the carcass from being stolen. Other big carnivores that live in the same area cannot climb trees so well as leopards. Once the prey is safe, a leopard can finish its meal.

Living Together

Most big cats live alone. They hunt alone and the females bring up their cubs alone. Big cats come together only when they want to mate. They are solitary because of the prey that they hunt. There is usually not enough prey in one area for a large group of big cats to live on. Lions are the exception. They live in family groups called prides. (Male cheetahs also sometimes live in groups with up to four members.) All wild cats have territories (home ranges). These territories are a series of trails that link together a cat's hunting area, its drinking places, its look-out positions and the den where it brings up its young. Females have smaller home ranges than males. Males that have more than one mate have territories that overlap with two or more female home ranges.

Did you know? Big cats' territories range from a few kilometres to over 1,000km /620 miles.

▲ BRINGING UP BABY

Female snow leopards bring up their cubs on their own. They have up to five cubs who stay with their mother for at least a year. Although snow leopards are loners, they are not unsociable. They like to live near each other and let other snow leopards cross their territories.

◄ THE LOOKOUT

A puma keeps watch over its territory from a hill. Pumas are solitary and deliberately avoid each other except during courtship and mating. The first male puma to arrive in an area claims it as his territory. He chases out any other male that tries to live there.

▲ A PRIDE OF LIONS

The lions in a pride drink together, hunt together, eat together and play together. A pride is usually made up of related females and their young. Prides usually try not to meet up with other prides. To tell the others to keep out of its territory, the pride leaves scent markings on the edge of its range.

Daniel and the Lions' Den
A story in the Bible tells how Daniel was taken prisoner by Nebuchadnezzar, king of Babylon. When Daniel correctly interpreted the king's dreams he became the king's friend. His enemies became jealous of his position and had him thrown into a lions' den, a common punishment for prisoners at the time. But instead of eating Daniel, the lions befriended him. They were tamed by his great faith in God.

▲ FAMILY GROUPS

A cheetah mother sits between her two cubs. The cubs will stay with her until they are about 18 months old. The female then lives a solitary life. Males, however, live in small groups and defend a territory. They only leave their range if there is a drought or if food is very scarce.

▲ WELL GROOMED

Cats that live together groom each other. They do this to be friendly and to keep clean. They also groom to spread their scent on each other, so that they smell the same. This helps them to recognize each other and identify strangers.

Focus on

Lions are the second largest of the big cats after tigers. They like to live in open spaces, sometimes in woodland, but never in tropical forests. Lions are usually found on the savanna (grassy plains) and on the edges of deserts. Female lions live together in prides (family groups) of up to 12 lionesses and their cubs. The size of the group depends on how much food there is available. Male lions may live together in groups, called coalitions, which look after one or more prides. The coalitions defend their prides, fighting off any other males who want to mate with the females of their pride.

FATHER AND SON

Male lions are the only big cats that look different from the females. Their long shaggy manes make them look larger and fiercer, and protect their necks in a fight. A male cub starts to grow a mane at about the age of three. At that age he also leaves the pride to establish his own territory.

THE FAMILY

A pride of lions rests near a waterhole. The biggest prides live in open grasslands where there are large herds of antelope, wildebeest and buffalo. If a foreign male takes over a pride, the new lion kills all the cubs under six months old. This is to make sure all the cubs are his.

a Pride

NURSERY SCHOOL

Young lions play tag to learn how to chase things and defend their pride. The pride does not usually allow strange lions to join the family group. Young lions need to be prepared in case other lions come to fight with them.

FIRST AT THE TABLE

Male lions usually eat first, even though the females do most of the hunting. A male can eat up to 30kg/65lb of meat at one time, but will not eat again for several days.

CAT SCRAP

Two lionesses fight each other to decide who will be first to eat. There is usually a dominant female in each pride, even when there are males around. This chief female rules the family.

MOTHER AND CUBS

Lionesses give birth to a litter of between one and six cubs. The cubs start learning to hunt when they are about 11 months old, but stay with their mother for over two years. In dry areas, lions live in small prides because less food is available.

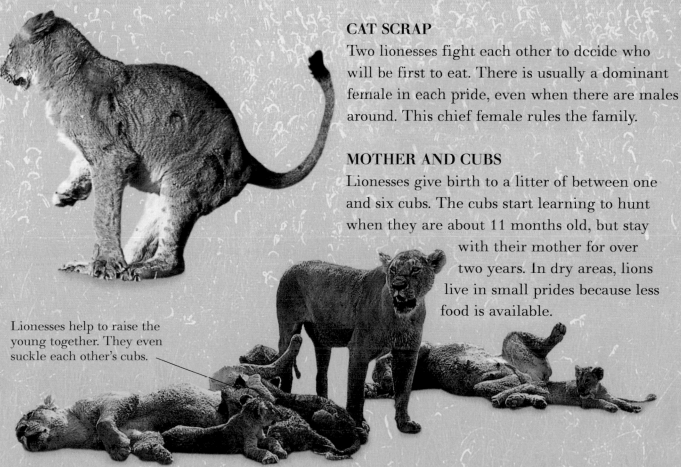

Lionesses help to raise the young together. They even suckle each other's cubs.

Finding a Mate

Big cats roam over large areas, so it can be quite difficult for them to find a partner. When they are ready to mate, they use scent markers. These are like advertisements to all the other cats in the district. A female also calls loudly in the hope that a nearby male will come to her. Often more than one male will follow a female. This almost always leads to fights between the interested males. The winner of the fight then begins to court the female. In a pride of lions, one male establishes his dominance over the group. In this way he avoids having to fight every time a female is ready to mate. Many big cats will mate several times a day for up to a week to make sure that the female is pregnant.

▲ COURTSHIP

A male lion rubs against a female and smells her all over. He knows that the lioness is ready to mate from her scent. Having fought off rivals, he must now persuade the lioness to mate with him. He courts her by being attentive. Their courtship may last for several days before they mate.

Did you know? Pumas are also called mountain screamers after the female's mating call.

◀ THE HAPPY COUPLE

When the female is ready to mate, she crouches on the ground with her hindquarters slightly raised. The male sits behind and over her and sometimes holds the scruff of her neck between his jaws. Large cats, such as lions, may mate up to 100 times in two days. Smaller cats, such as cheetahs, are more vulnerable to predators and so mate for a shorter time.

KEEPING HIM IN HIS PLACE ▶

After mating, the lioness is aggressive and often lashes out at the lion. As soon as the two have mated the male jumps back very quickly. He remains close by her side to stop other males from approaching. Once she has calmed down, she rolls on her back and they mate again. Each mating lasts only a few seconds.

Did you know? A wild big cat may have up to 5 litters in an average lifespan of 12 years.

▼ ANIMAL ATTRACTION

Two courting tigers often make a great deal of noise. They roar, meow, moan and grunt as they mate. Female tigers mate every other year. The male stays close by the female for a few days until he is sure she is pregnant. Then the pair separate and live on their own again.

▲ LEAN AND HEALTHY

This lioness is only just pregnant. She has not put on much weight and can still hunt efficiently. At the end of her pregnancy (about three to four months) she will hunt small, easy-to-catch prey. Lionesses in a pride also get to share in the pride's kill.

Giving Birth

The cubs (babies) of a big cat are usually born with spotted fur and closed eyes. They are completely helpless. The mother cat looks after them on her own with no help from the father. She gives birth in a safe place called a den. For the first few days after birth, she stays very close to her cubs so that they can feed on her milk. She keeps them warm and cleans the cubs by licking them all over. The cubs grow quickly. Even before their eyes open they can crawl, and they soon learn to hiss to defend themselves.

▲ SNOW CUB

Snow leopard cubs have white fur with dark spots. They are always born in the spring and open their eyes one week after birth. The cubs begin to follow their mothers around when they are about three months old. By winter, they will be almost grown up.

MOTHERLY LOVE ▶

Tiger cubs are capable killers by the time they are 11 months old. They stay with their mothers, however, until they are two or even three years of age. In the wild, the mother does all she can to protect her young, but often at least half of the litter dies. Predators may kill the cubs or sometimes they starve to death if the mother cannot catch enough food.

IN DISGUISE ▶

A cheetah cub is covered in long, woolly fur. This makes it look similar to the African honey badger, a very fierce animal, which may help to discourage predators. The mother cheetah does not raise her cubs in a den, but moves them around every few days.

A cheetah cub, unlike the adult, has a mane of fur. This may help to disguise it as it hides in the long grass.

▲ BRINGING UP BABY

Female pumas give birth to up to six kittens (babies). The mother has several pairs of teats for the kittens to suckle from. Each kitten has its own teat and will use no other. They will suckle her milk for at least three months and from about six weeks they will also eat meat.

▲ ON GUARD

Two lionesses guard the entrance to their den. Lions are social cats and share the responsibility of keeping guard. Dens are kept very clean so that there are no smells to attract predators.

▲ MOVING TO SAFETY

If at any time a mother cat thinks her cubs are in danger, she will move them to a new den. She carries the cubs one by one, gently grasping the loose skin at their necks between her teeth.

37

Focus on

PLAY TIME
A cub plays with its mother's tail. As soon as cubs can see, they begin to play. Play helps to build up muscles, improve co-ordination and develop good reflexes. It is valuable early preparation for learning how to hunt when the cubs are older.

The number of cubs in a big cat's litter depends on the species and where it lives. Most big cats have two or three cubs, but cheetahs have five or more. All cubs are born helpless, but it is not long before their eyes open and they can wobble around, learning to balance on their uncertain legs. Within a few weeks they begin to play with their mothers and each other. There is a lot to find out, but they learn very quickly. By the time they are six months old they will have learned how to keep themselves safe, what food tastes good and how to catch it. They will start to understand the language of smells and sounds. For the next year and a half they will stay close to their mothers, perfecting their new skills.

SAFETY FIRST
For the first two years of their lives, cubs remain close to their mothers. She protects them and helps them when they make mistakes. A mother may rear all of her cubs successfully in a good year. She may lose most or even all of her cubs, depending on her skills as a parent and the availability of food.

BATH TIME
Cubs must learn to clean themselves, but while they are still young their mother washes them with her tongue. As she licks, she spreads her scent on the cubs so that all of her family have the same smell.

Cute Cubs

FAMILY BLISS

Lion cubs are spotted all over to help hide them from predators. The spots gradually fade as the lions grow older. Adult lions have only very faint spots on their legs and stomachs. Lion cubs are lucky because they have many companions to play with. Cubs of solitary cats have to grow up without much company. Some do not even have any brothers or sisters. Lion cubs learn through play how to get along with other lions.

MOVING HOME

To move her cubs a lioness carries each one gently in her mouth. Not only do the cubs have loose skin at their necks, but the lioness has a special gap in her mouth behind the canines. This allows her to lift the cub off the ground without biting it.

LION LESSONS

These cubs are working together to kill an injured warthog. One grabs the neck, while the other starts tearing at the hind leg. The mother lioness watches over them. She is the cubs' teacher. They must learn to hunt as soon as possible, and this warthog is a small animal for them to begin with. The lioness brought down the warthog so that the cubs could learn to kill it.

Growing Up

Growing cubs have to learn all about life as an adult so that they can look after themselves when they leave their mother. She teaches them as much as she can and the rest they learn through play. Cub games depend on their species, because each type of cat has different things to learn. In playfighting cheetahs use their paws to knock each other over. This is a technique they will need for hunting when they are older. Cubs need to learn how to judge distances and when to strike to kill prey quickly, without getting injured or killed themselves. Their mother introduces them to prey by bringing an animal back to the den to eat. Mothers and cubs use very high-pitched sounds to communicate. However, if she senses danger, she growls at them to tell them to hide.

▲ PRACTICE MAKES PERFECT
These cheetah cubs are learning to kill a Thomson's gazelle. When the cubs are about 12 weeks old, a mother cheetah brings back live injured prey for them to kill. They instinctively know how to do so, but need practice to get it right.

▼ FOLLOW MY LEADER
Curious cheetah cubs watch an object intently, safe beside their mother. At about six weeks the cubs start to go on hunting trips with her. They are able to keep up by following her white-tipped tail through the tall grass.

THE CLASSROOM ▶

A group of lion cubs relaxes in the shade on a fallen tree. From here they watch the adults hunt, as if in a big, open-air classroom. Female cubs often stay in the pride, but young males are chased off by the dominant male.

◀ SCRATCH AND SNIFF

Three young lions sniff at the shell of a tortoise. Cubs learn to be cautious when dealing with unfamiliar objects. First the object is tapped with a paw, before being explored further with the nose. Cubs' milk teeth are replaced with permanent canine teeth at about two years old. Not until then can they begin to hunt and kill big animals.

TAIL TOY ▶

A mother leopard's tail is a good thing for her cub to learn to pounce on. She twitches it so the cub can develop good co-ordination and timing. As the cub grows, it will try out on rodents and then bigger animals until it can hunt for itself. Once they leave their mothers, female cubs usually establish a territory close by, while males go farther away.

Enemies of Big Cats

Big cats are perfect killing machines and are feared by all their prey. They do, however, have enemies. Big cats have to watch out for other carnivores taking their food or attacking their cubs. Wolves are a problem for pumas, wild dogs are a threat to tigers, and hyenas and jackals prey on the cubs of African big cats. Even prey animals can be a danger to big cats. Buffaloes are very aggressive and can attack and kill a young lion. Humans, however, are the main enemies of wild cats. As people move farther into the wilderness to build homes and farms, they destroy the precious habitats of the big cats. People kill the big cats' prey, leaving them with less to eat. They also hunt big cats for their beautiful and valuable fur coats.

▲ **SCAVENGING HYENAS**
A spotted hyena finishes off the remains of a giraffe. Hyenas live in Africa and western Asia. They eat whatever they can find. This is often carrion (the remains of dead prey) that animals such as big cats have killed for themselves. They will also kill cubs. Hyenas have strong jaws and bone-crunching teeth and look for food at night.

Did you know? Despite their dog-like appearance, hyenas are more closely related to cats.

◄ **PACK POWER**
Wolves live in Europe and North America. They live in the mountains as well as on open plains and hunt in packs of up to 20 animals. Wolves usually eat deer, elk, moose or small animals such as hares.

BIG CAT THREAT ▶

Leopards live in the same areas as cheetahs, but they are very hostile towards them. In fact, if they get a chance, leopards prey on cheetahs and their cubs. In turn, leopards have to be very wary of lions. Lions will attack and kill a leopard to protect the pride or their territory. Big cats do not like others because of competition for food in an area.

▼ **DOG-LIKE JACKALS**

Jackals (a relative of the dog) are half the size of hyenas and live in Africa. They will eat most things and will steal a big cat's kill. If they come across an unprotected den, they quickly kill and eat all the cubs.

▲ **HUMAN TRAPS**

Experts examine a tiger trap. Poachers (people who kill animals illegally) often use traps to catch big cats. When the trap snaps shut, the animal is stuck until it dies or until the poacher returns to kill it. These traps cause great pain. A cat may try to chew off its trapped leg to escape.

◀ **INTRUDER PERIL**

Sometimes big cats become cannibals and eat their own kind. These cheetahs are eating another cheetah that has invaded their territory. Male lions also eat all the young cubs in a pride when they take over dominance from another male.

Mountain Cats

To live in the mountains, cats need to be hardy and excellent rock climbers. They also have to cope with high altitudes where the air is thin and there is less oxygen to breathe. Big cats that live in the mountains include leopards and the rare snow leopard. Small cats include the puma, mountain cat, bobcat and lynx. Mountain climates are harsh and the weather can change very quickly. To survive, mountain cats need to use their wits and to know where to find shelter. They mate so that their cubs are born in the spring. This is to make sure that they will be almost grown by the time winter closes in.

▲ **MOUNTAIN CAT**
The mountain cat is a secretive, shy creature and seldom seen. It is about 50cm/20in long and has soft, fine fur. It is also known as the Andean mountain cat, since it lives in the Andes mountains of Chile, Argentina, Peru and Bolivia. This cat is found at altitudes of up to 5,000m/ 16,500ft above sea level.

This map shows the world's major mountain ranges. The puma, mountain cat and lynx live in the Americas. Lynx also live in Europe and Asia, while the snow leopard lives in Asia.

◄ **MOUNTAIN LION**
A puma keeps watch over its vast territory. Pumas are also known as mountain lions and cougars. Male pumas can grow to 2m/6½ft long, and weigh 100kg/ 220lb. They are good at jumping and can easily leap 5m/16ft on to a high rock or into a tree. Pumas are found over a wide area, from Canada to the very tip of South America. They live along the foothills of mountains, in forests on mountain slopes and all the way up to 4,500m/ 14,800ft above sea level.

WINTER LYNX ▶

Lynx live in
mountainous
regions of Europe,
Asia and North
America. They have
unusually short tails
and tufted ears. Lynx are
well designed to live in very
cold places. In winter they
grow an especially long coat,
which is pale so that they are
well camouflaged in
the snow. The bobcat of
North America looks
similar to the lynx.

◀ **PUMA CHASE**

A snowshoe hare darts this
way and that to shake off a
puma. To catch the hare, the
puma must make full use of
its flexible back and its long
balancing tail. Pumas hunt
by day as well as by night.

LONG-TAILED SNOW LEOPARD ▶

The snow leopard is one of the rarest big cats. It is
found only in the Himalaya and Altai mountains of
central Asia. It can live at altitudes of 6,000m/
19,700ft, the highest of any wild cat. Snow
leopards feed on wild goats, hares (jack rabbits)
and marmots. Their bodies measure just over
1m/1yd long, with tails that are almost as long.
They wrap their bushy tails around themselves
to keep warm when they are
sleeping. Snow leopards are agile
jumpers and are said to be able
to leap a gap of 15m/49ft.
Their long tails help
them to balance as
they jump.

Did you know? A female snow leopard makes her den cosy by lining it with her own fur.

45

Forest Dwellers

Dense, wet rainforests are home to lots of small creatures, such as insects and spiders. These animals and forest plants provide a feast for birds, snakes, frogs and small mammals, which in turn are a banquet for big cats. Jaguars, tigers, leopards and clouded leopards all live in rainforests. Small cats include ocelots and margays. Although there is plenty of food in a forest, the dense trees make it a difficult place to hunt. There is little space among the trees and prey can escape easily in the thick undergrowth.

▲ **CLOUDED LEOPARD**

The clouded leopard is a shy and rarely seen Asian big cat. It lives in forests from Nepal to Borneo, spending most of its time in the trees. The Chinese call the clouded leopard the mint leopard because of its unusual leaf-like markings. Male clouded leopards reach about 1m/1yd long, with an equally long tail, and weigh about 30kg/65lb. They are perfectly built for tree climbing, with a long, bushy tail for balance and flexible ankle joints.

This map shows where the world's tropical rainforests are located. They lie in a band on either side of the Equator.

JAGUAR ▼

Although jaguars live in grasslands and semi-deserts, they prefer the thick forests of South and Central America. They are the third largest big cat, growing to 2.4m/7¾ft in length and weighing up to 120kg/265lb.

Did you know? The jaguar was the symbol of the Sun for the Maya of Central America.

The sleek margay is very striking in appearance, with beautifully marked fur and large eyes.

▲ SUMATRAN TIGER

A tiger walks stealthily into a jungle pool on the island of Sumatra. Tigers are good swimmers and a forest pool is a good place to hunt as well as to cool off from the tropical heat. Tigers often hide the carcasses of their prey in water or the dense undergrowth.

▲ MARGAY

Margays live in the tropical forests of Central and South America. They are the best of all cat climbers, with broad, soft feet and exceptionally flexible ankles and hind legs. They feed largely on birds and so need to be good at moving around in the tops of trees.

▲ JAVAN LEOPARD

At one time, many leopards lived in the tropical rainforests of Asia. But now, like this Javan leopard, they are endangered. They are threatened by over-hunting and the destruction of their forest habitat.

◄ BLACK JAGUAR

Forest jaguars are darker than their grassland cousins. Some can be black and are so well camouflaged that they can disappear in the shadows of their forest habitat.

▲ A TURTLE TREAT

A jaguar catches a river turtle in a pool. Jaguars are such good swimmers that they hunt some of their prey in water. They love to eat fish and turtles. Their jaws are powerful enough to crack open a turtle's shell like a nut. They have been known to kill cayman (a type of crocodile).

Focus on

Tigers are the largest of all the big cats, and the largest of all tigers is the Siberian tiger. An adult male can reach up to 2.6m/8½ft long and weigh as much as 270kg/600lb. Siberian tigers live in the snow-covered forests of Siberia, which is part of Russia, and in Manchuria in China. They are also sometimes known as Amur tigers. Although there is only one species of tiger, they can differ significantly in their appearance. Siberian tigers have a relatively pale coat with few stripes. Bengal tigers from India, however, have shorter fur and are more strikingly marked. As humans destroy more of their habitats, the number of tigers in the wild is declining dramatically. Today, there are only about 400 Siberian tigers left in the wild.

SOLITARY SIBERIAN

Siberian tigers live alone in huge territories of over 1,000 square km/400 square miles. They do not like to fight, but a tiger will kill another if it invades its territory.

OPEN WIDE

A Siberian tiger shows its long, sharp canine teeth in a wide yawn. Canines are used to catch and kill prey. Tigers ambush prey and kill it by biting the neck or strangling it.

LUNCH TIME

A group of Siberian tigers devours a black ox. Despite being solitary animals, tigers do sometimes share food. The only other time they come together is to mate. Tigers have been known to roar when they have killed a big animal, just as lions will often roar when they have successfully caught their prey.

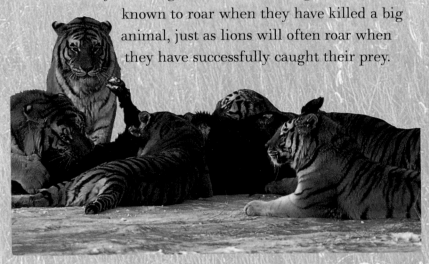

Siberian Tigers

ICY TONIC
A mother shows her 18-month-old cub how to get water from melted ice. Tigers have up to four cubs in a litter, every other year. They stay with her for at least two years.

COURTING COUPLE
When a female is ready to mate, she sprays, roars and grunts to tell the male. When tigers want to be friendly, they blow sharply through their nostrils and mouths, rub their heads together and gently bite each other's necks.

A PALE ICE QUEEN
Siberian tigers, like this female, have a lot of white fur. This makes it more difficult for prey and enemies to see them in the snow. They are powerfully and heavily built, with bodies slung close to the ground.

On the Savanna

Savannas are open, flat areas of grassland. Apart from grasses, the main plants of the savanna are small bushes and clumps of trees. Savanna is the ideal habitat for big herds of grazing animals, such as antelope, zebra and buffalo. In Africa, these herds migrate for thousands of kilometres each year in search of fresh grass and water. They are followed by lions, cheetahs and leopards who prey on the herds. The savanna of South America is home to jaguars. Rodents, such as mice, gerbils and marmots, also thrive on the savanna and these are a good food source for smaller cats, such as the serval.

▲ LION IN THE GRASS
A lion walks through the long, dry grass of the African savanna. Its sandy coloration perfectly matches its habitat. Lions hunt their quarry using the cover of grass. Often, only the tips of a lion's ears are seen as it slowly stalks its prey.

This map shows where the world's savannas (tropical grasslands and dry woodlands) are located. The largest region of savanna lies in Africa.

Did you know? Cats sleep for longer than most other animals. Lions sleep for 20 hours a day.

◀ CHEETAH ON THE LOOKOUT
A cheetah stands on the top of a small mound on the Kenyan savanna. Cheetahs are perfectly adapted for life on the plains. The surrounding open, flat terrain lets them make the most of their ability to chase down prey. From its vantage point, a cheetah uses its excellent eyesight to search for prey. It also keeps watch for any other cheetahs who might have invaded its home range.

◄ VIEW FROM A BRANCH

Leopards like to live in areas of grassland where there are trees. Here they can sleep hidden during the heat of the day. They can also enjoy the afternoon breeze and avoid the insects that live in the grass below. Leopards also prefer to eat up in a tree, out of the reach of scavengers.

Leo the Lion
People born between July 24 and August 23 are born under the astrological sign of Leo (the lion.) They are said to be brave, strong and proud, just like lions.

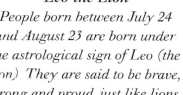

▲ AT THE WATERHOLE

During the dry season in the African savanna, many grazing animals gather near waterholes to drink. Thomson's gazelle, zebra and giraffe are shown here. Lions congregate around the waterholes, not only to drink, but also to catch prey unawares. Their preferred prey is antelope, buffalo, zebra and warthog, but they also eat giraffe.

SPEEDY SERVAL ►

Servals are small cats that live on the savanna of western and central Africa. They like to live near water where there are bushes to hide in. The servals' long legs enable them to leap over tall grass when they hunt small rodents. They also climb well and hunt birds. With their long legs, servals can run quickly over short distances and so escape from predators.

51

Desert Cats

Hot deserts are very dry places. Although they are hot during the day, at night they are very cold. Few plants and animals can survive in such a harsh environment, but cats are very adaptable. Cheetahs, lions and leopards live in the Kalahari and Namib deserts of southern Africa. As long as there are animals to eat, the cats can survive. Even the jaguar, a cat that loves water, has been seen in desert areas in Mexico and the southern United States. But they are only visitors in this tough, dry land and soon go back to the wetter places they prefer. The best-adapted cat to desert life is a small variety known as the sand cat. It lives in the northern Sahara Desert, the Middle East and western Asia.

Did you know? Lions follow along dry riverbeds looking for waterholes in the desert.

▲ **DESERT STORM**
Two lions endure a sandstorm in the Kalahari Desert of southern Africa. The desert is a very hostile place to live. There is very little water, not much food and the wind blows up terrible sandstorms. Despite these hardships, big cats, such as these lions, manage to survive.

This map shows where the world's hot deserts and nearby semi-desert areas are located.

▼ **A HARSH LIFE**
An old lion drinks from a waterhole in the Kalahari Desert. Even when a big cat lives in a dry place, it still needs to find enough water to drink. This is often a difficult task, requiring the animals to walk long distances. In the desert, prey is usually very spread out, so an old lion has a hard time trying to feed itself adequately.

▲ CHEETAH WALK

A group of cheetahs walk across the wide expanse of the Kalahari Desert. They lead lives of feast and famine. In the rainy season, lush vegetation grows and enormous herds of antelope can graze. The cheetahs have a banquet preying on the grazing herds. But they go very hungry as the land dries up and prey becomes scarce.

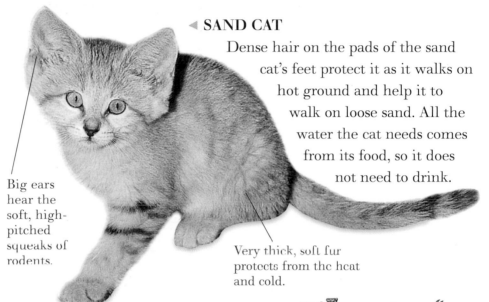

Big ears hear the soft, high-pitched squeaks of rodents.

◄ SAND CAT

Dense hair on the pads of the sand cat's feet protect it as it walks on hot ground and help it to walk on loose sand. All the water the cat needs comes from its food, so it does not need to drink.

Very thick, soft fur protects from the heat and cold.

▲ ADAPTABLE LEOPARD

A leopard rolls in the desert sand. There are very few trees in the desert, so leopards live among rocky outcrops. Here they can drag their prey to high places to eat in safety. The desert can be a dangerous place. With so little food around, competition can be fierce, especially with hungry lions. Big cats will eat small prey such as insects to keep from starving.

Egyptian Cat Worship
The Ancient Egyptians kept cats to protect their stores of grain from rats and mice. Cats became so celebrated that they were worshipped as gods. They were sacred to the cat-headed goddess of pleasure, Bast. Many cats were given funerals when they died. Their bodies were preserved, wrapped in bandages and richly painted.

53

Killer Cats

Humans can sometimes become the prey of big cats. People have been afraid of big cats for thousands of years. From 20,000-year-old cave paintings we know that people lived in contact with big cats and almost certainly feared them. More recently, there have been many reports of big cats killing people. Lions and tigers become bold when they are hungry and there is little other food around. First, they prey on livestock, such as cattle. When the cattle are gone, the big cats might kill people. Leopards, who do not have a natural fear of humans, may have their killer instinct triggered by an injury.

▲ LION BAITING

The Romans used lions (and bears) for gladiator fights in their amphitheatres (outdoor arenas). When the Romans wanted to kill prisoners, they would feed them to hungry lions. The lions had to be starving and made angry by their handlers, otherwise they would not kill the prisoners. Most captive lions will not kill people.

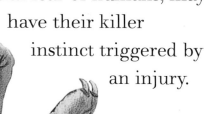

◄ WRESTLING A TIGER

Tigers are considered the most dangerous of all the big cats. This picture, called *A Timely Rescue*, shows a rather heroic view of killing a tiger. Once a tiger has become used to the taste of human flesh, it will strike at any time. Tigers have killed thousands of people over the centuries. During the early 20th century, tigers killed 800 to 900 people a year in India.

Did you know? In the early 20th century, one Indian leopard killed 125 people in eight years.

▲ TIPPU'S TIGER

This mechanical toy of a tiger attacking a British soldier was made in 1790. It is called Tippu's Tiger and was made for the Sultan of Mysore. The Sultan resisted the British takeover of India, and his toy makes growling and screaming noises.

◄ HUNTER WITH A HEART

Jim Corbett was a famous hunter who lived in India in the early 20th century. Unlike most hunters of his day, he did not kill big cats for sport. He shot tigers and leopards that had been eating people.

Jaguar Knights

In the 1500s in Central America, Aztec warriors were divided into military orders. Some of the most prestigious were the jaguar knights who ranked just below the emperor. They wore entire wild cats' pelts, with the still-attached heads worn as helmets. They thought that by wearing the pelt they would take on the cat's strength and stealth.

▲ EDUCATION FOR CONSERVATION

Around 100 tigers and 50 leopards live in the Corbett National Park in India. The Park runs classes to teach children all about the big cats and their habitat. The more we know about big cats, the better able we are to respect them.

Cats in Danger

The earliest record that we have of people using wild-cat pelts (skins) is from 6500BC. It comes from the archaeological site of Çatal Hüyük in Turkey where there is evidence that dancers wore leopard skins. Much more recently, in the 19th and 20th centuries, many wealthy people wanted to hunt big game for the thrill of the chase. Big cat skins were used to decorate the hunters' houses, and their heads hung as trophies on the walls. Today, no one is allowed to hunt the endangered big cats anymore.

▲ LION HUNT
Egyptian rulers hunted lions from horse-drawn chariots. Hieroglyphics (picture writing) tell us of Pharaoh Amenophis III (1405–1367BC) who killed over 100 lions in the ten years of his rule. Some experts now think that the Egyptians may have bred lions specially to hunt them.

TIGER-HUNTING PRINCE ▶
This old painting on cotton shows an Indian prince hunting a tiger from the back of his elephant. Tiger hunting was a very popular pastime for many centuries in India until it was declared illegal in the 1970s.

▼ **GREAT WHITE HUNTER**
A hunting party proudly displays its tiger trophy. This photograph was taken in the 1860s. When India was under British rule, tiger hunting was considered to be a great sport by the British. Uncontrolled, ruthless hunting was a major cause of the tiger's dramatic fall in numbers.

▲ **RITUAL ROBES**
The Zulu chief Mangosothu Buthelezi wears wild cat skins on special occasions, like many African leaders and tribal healers. They are a sign of his rank and high status.

Did you know? Until the 19th century, black panthers lived near Los Angeles, California.

◄ **CAT'S SKIN**
A leopard is skinned, having been shot in the Okavango Delta in Botswana. Some game reserves raise money for conservation by charging huge sums to hunt. This only happens when numbers of a certain species are too large for the reserve.

SECOND SKIN ►
Some people continue to think it looks good to wear a coat made from the pelts of a wild cat. Many more, however, think that the fur looks much better on the cat. Designers now use fake fur and skins dyed to look like pelts, instead.

Big Cat Relatives

Fossil remains show that the ancestors of today's cats first roamed the earth 65 million years ago. They were small animals called miacids. Scientists think that the miacids may be the forerunners of all carnivorous mammals on Earth today. About 35 million years ago the first cat-like carnivores appeared. Many of these early cats were large and dangerous creatures that have now become extinct (died out). The best-known are the sabre-toothed cats, which, unlike modern cats, used their canines for stabbing rather than biting. Fossil records of cats very similar to modern cats date back about 10 million years. Today, there are 39 species of wild cat, big and small, and over 300 breeds of domestic cat.

▲ **ANCIENT ANCESTOR**

Miacids are thought to have been the first true carnivorous mammals. They first lived about 65 million years ago, around the same time that the dinosaurs died out. They are the first animals to have carnassial teeth – the strong back teeth used for shearing meat.

Did you know? The bones of sabre-toothed cats have been found under Trafalgar Square, London.

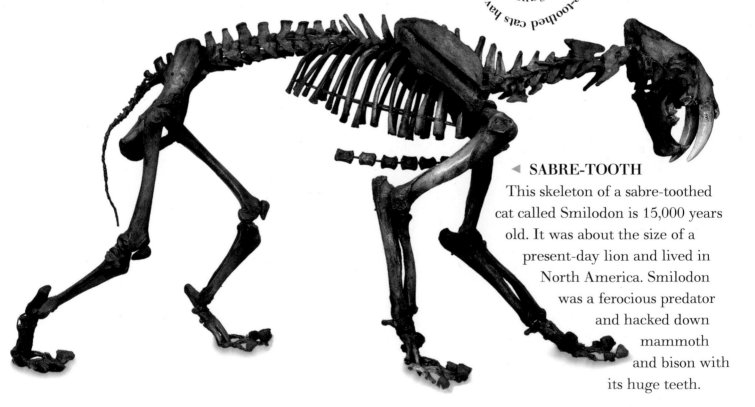

◄ **SABRE-TOOTH**

This skeleton of a sabre-toothed cat called Smilodon is 15,000 years old. It was about the size of a present-day lion and lived in North America. Smilodon was a ferocious predator and hacked down mammoth and bison with its huge teeth.

◄ DOMESTIC CATS

Small cats are grouped under the genus *Felis*. Domestic or pet cats (*Felis catus*) are like miniature tamed versions of their wild relatives the big cats. They hunt, groom and leave scent marks just like wild cats. When a house cat rubs itself against a human, it is showing affection, but also putting its smell on that person.

Classification Chart

Kingdom	**Animalia**	(all animals)
Phylum	**Chordata**	(animals with backbones)
Class	**Mammalia**	(animals with hair on their bodies that feed their young with milk)
Order	**Carnivora**	(mammals that eat meat)
Family	**Felidae**	(all cats)
Genus	*Panthera*	(big cats)
Species	*leo*	(lion)

▲ CAT NAMES

Scientists classify (group) every cat within the animal kingdom and give it a Latin name. This chart shows how the lion is classified.

SERVAL ►

The serval (*Felis serval*) is a spotted, fleet-footed wild cat. It lives near water in southern and central Africa. Although it has long legs like a cheetah, it belongs to a different group and purrs like a domestic cat.

CARACAL ►

The caracal's (*Felis caracal*) most startling feature is the long tufts on its ears. These may help it to locate prey. The caracal is related to both the leopard and the lynx. It lives in grasslands, open woodland and scrub in Africa and parts of Asia.

BOBCAT ►

The bobcat (*Felis rufus*) is related to the lynx (*Felis lynx*). Both have short tails and live in many sorts of habitats, but prefer the rocks and shrubby plants of mountain slopes. The bobcat is only found in northern North America where it is able to survive the harsh winter conditions.

Protecting Cats

All big cats are in danger of extinction. They are hunted not only for their skins, but also for their teeth, bones and other body parts, which are used as traditional medicines in many countries. The Convention for International Trade in Endangered Species (CITES) lists all big cats under Appendix 1, which strictly controls their import and export. For cats particularly at risk, such as the tiger, all trade is banned. There are now many protected areas throughout the world where big cats can live without human interference. These areas are often not big enough, however, so the cats leave in search of food. They attack livestock and sometimes the local farmers.

▲ IN ANCIENT TIMES

A Roman mosaic showing a horseman hunting a leopard. Two thousand years ago, big cats were much more widespread. Until the 1900s, cheetahs lived throughout Africa, central India and the Middle East. Hunting big cats was not a problem when there were many big cats and not so many people, but now the situation is desperate.

▲ GIR NATIONAL PARK

The last remaining Asiatic lions live in the Gir Forest National Park in India. There are only around 400 lions in the park, though numbers are increasing. The Asiatic lion is slightly different to the African lion. It has a smaller mane and a fold of skin running between its front and back legs.

▲ SERENGETI LION PROJECT

This lion has been drugged so that it can be fitted with a radio collar, checked and then released. In the Serengeti National Park in Tanzania, scientists use methods like this to study how lions behave.

▼ RADIO TRACKING

Biologists attach a radio collar to a tigress in the Chitwan National Park in Nepal. To save wild cats we need to understand their habits and their needs. For this reason, many scientists and conservationists are studying them. It is a very difficult task since cats are secretive and often nocturnal animals. One way of gathering information is to put a radio collar on a big cat and then follow its movements. By doing this, the animal can be tracked at long range.

▲ TIGER DETERRENT

Villagers in the Sundarbans mangrove forests in India wear masks on the backs of their heads. Tigers attack from behind, but will not usually strike if they see a face. The largest remaining tiger population in India is in the Sundarbans. Here 50 to 60 people die each year from attacks by tigers. There is obviously not enough food for the tigers, so conservationists are trying to improve the situation. Another deterrent is to set up dummies that look and smell like humans, but give out an electric shock if attacked. There are also electrified fences in some areas, and pigs are bred and released as tiger food.

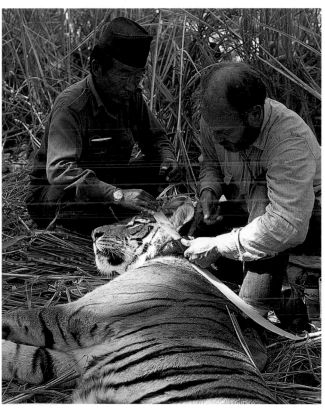

The Great Sphinx

In Egypt, an enormous statue with a human head and the body of a lion guards the Great Pyramids at Giza. This statue is the Great Sphinx. A story written in 1419BC on the Sphinx tells of a prince called Thutmose IV who fell asleep between the paws of the statue. He dreamt that the Sun god told him to take away the sand covering part of the Sphinx and he would become a king. When he awoke, Thutmose did as he had been instructed, and the dream came true.

GLOSSARY

altitude
The height of a place given in metres (or feet) above sea level.

ambush
When an animal hides, waiting for prey to walk past, then pounces on it in a surprise attack.

artery
A blood vessel that carries blood away from the heart.

binocular vision
The ability to see things with both eyes at the same time. This enables cats to judge distances and depth accurately.

bladder
Where waste urine is stored in the body before being expelled.

breed
An animal that belongs to one species, but has definite characteristics, such as coloration, body shape and coat markings.

camouflage
Coloration or patterns that allow an animal to blend in with its surroundings to avoid detection.

canines
The sharp, pointed teeth that cats use for killing and holding prey.

carnassials
The strong, shearing teeth at the back of a cat's mouth.

carnivore
An animal that feeds mainly on the flesh of other animals.

classification
Arranging animals according to their similarities and differences in order to study them and suggest how they may be related.

dew claw
The digit (toe) on a cat's front foot that is held off the ground to keep it sharp. It is used to knock down and hold on to prey.

digestion
The process by which food is broken down so that it can be absorbed by the body.

domestic cat
A species of cat whose wild ancestors were tamed by people and bred in captivity.

dominance
A system between social big cats, such as lions, in which one or a few animals rule the group. The rulers have first choice over the other, more junior members.

Equator
An imaginary line running around the Earth like a belt, separating north from south.

evolve
When an animal or plant species develops and changes over a long time. As conditions alter, living things change to become better adapted (suited) to surviving. Those that cannot adapt may go extinct (die out completely).

extinct
When a whole species or larger group of animals or plants has disappeared, dying out completely.

fossil
The remains of a once-living plant or animal that have turned to stone over thousands or millions of years.

gland
An organ in the body that produces chemicals for a particular use.

habitat
A type of living area that has certain kinds of animals and plants living there, such as tropical rainforest or semi-desert.

incisors
The front teeth, which a cat uses for cutting up meat.

insulation
A covering, like a cat's fur coat, that does not allow too much heat in or out of the body.

intestine
Part of the gut of an animal specialized to digest food.

jungle
The dense undergrowth found in a rainforest.

kidney
An organ of the body that filters blood to remove waste products, called urine.

liver
An organ that processes food from the digestive system (gut). One of the liver's main tasks is to remove any poisons from the blood.

lungs
An organ of the body that takes in oxygen from the air.

mammal
A warm-blooded animal that has an internal skeleton, a fur-covered body and mammary glands that produce milk to feed its babies.

mangrove
Trees that grow in muddy swamps near the sea.

mating
The pairing up of a male and female to produce young. During mating, the fertilization (joining together) of a male sperm and a female egg takes place, which starts a new life.

membrane
A thin layer of skin that separates one area from another.

milk teeth
A young animal's first teeth, which are replaced by permanent teeth.

nerves
Fibres that carry electrical impulses to and from the brain.

oesophagus
Part of the gut of an animal, usually long and tube-shaped. It transports swallowed food from the mouth to the stomach.

predator
An animal that catches and kills other animals (prey) for its food.

prey
An animal that is hunted for food by another animal (predator).

rainforest
A tropical forest where it is hot and wet all year round.

rodent
An animal with chisel-shaped incisors (front teeth), used for gnawing. Rats, mice, beavers and porcupines are all types of rodent.

savanna
Open grasslands with a few scattered trees in tropical regions.

scavenger
An animal that feeds mainly on the remains left behind from another animal's meal.

social animal
An animal that lives in a group, usually with others of its own kind. Social animals co-operate with other group members.

species
All living things are grouped into species. Animals of the same species are similar to each other and can breed with each other. They produce young that in turn can breed together. All lions belong to one species, tigers to another and leopards to another. Each species is given a unique name, usually in Latin.

The species name for lions is *Panthera leo*, for tigers it is *Panthera tigris* and for leopards it is *Panthera pardus*.

stalk
To follow prey quietly and carefully so that a predator is within striking distance.

sweat glands
Small organs beneath an animal's skin that produce sweat. Sweat helps to keep the body cool.

taste buds
Tiny bumps on an animal's tongue, which have nerve endings that pick up taste signals.

territory
An area in which an animal or group of animals live. Cats use scent to mark the borders of their territories so that other cats know to keep out.

trachea
The windpipe running from the nose and mouth used to transport air to the lungs.

tropics
Warm, wet regions of the Earth that lie near the Equator.

vein
A blood vessel that carries blood back toward the heart.

warm-blooded
An animal that is able to maintain its body temperature at the same level all the time.

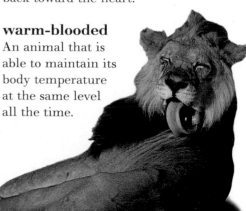

INDEX

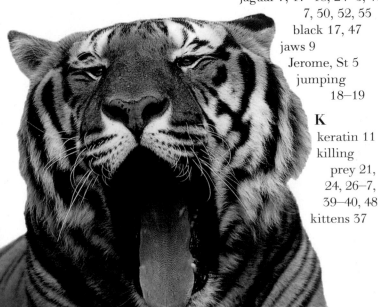